JUST FOR FUN

CHILDREN'S SONGS FOR UKULELE

59 CHILDREN'S CLASSICS
ARRANGED BY DICK SHERIDAN

Produced by
Alfred Music
P.O. Box 10003
Van Nuys, CA 91410-0003
alfred.com

Printed in USA.

ISBN-10: 0-7390-9625-7
ISBN-13: 978-0-7390-9625-3

Cover Photos
Central image models: Katrina Hruschka and Andrew Callahan / Photographer: Brian Immke, www.adeptstudios.com
3 Cherry uke: courtesy of C.F. Martin & Co • Moon: courtesy of The Library of Congress • Gramophone: © istockphoto / Faruk
MP3 player: © istockphoto / tpopova • Microphone: © istockphoto / Graffizone • Handstand: © istockphoto / jhorrock
Jumping woman: © istockphoto / Dan Wilton • Woman and radio: courtesy of The Library of Congress • Sneakers: © istockphoto /
Background: image copyright Elise Gravel, 2009, used under license from Shutterstock.com

 Alfred Cares. Contents printed on 100% recycled paper.

FOREWORD

This book is designed to be playable by beginning and novice
musicians. It's perfect for children, and for parents who want
to strum and sing these great songs along with their kids.
Plus, matching guitar, mandolin, and banjo books are available—
just for fun!

—Aaron Stang, Director Pop and Classroom Guitar
Alfred Music

CONTENTS

A-B-C	4
A-Hunting We Will Go	5
All the Pretty Little Horses	6
All Through the Night	7
The Alphabet Song	8
Angels Watching Over Me	9
The Animal Fair	10
Baa, Baa, Black Sheep	11
The Bear Climbed Over the Mountain	12
Bill Hogan's Goat	13
Billy Boy	14
Bingo	15
Blue Jay Pulled the Four-Horse Plow	16
Bobby Shafto	17
Brahms' Lullaby	18
Come Little Leaves	19
Did You Ever See a Lassie?	20
Do Your Ears Hang Low?	21
The Farmer in the Dell	22
Father's Whiskers	23
Found a Peanut	24
Frère Jacques	26
Go In and Out the Window	25
Goodbye, My Lover, Goodbye	28
Goodnight, Ladies	30
Here We Go 'Round the Mulberry Bush	31
Hickory Dickory Dock	32
Hush, Little Baby	33
I Have a Little Dreidel	34
If You're Happy (And You Know It)	35
It's Raining, It's Pouring	36
Itsy Bitsy Spider	37
Jesus Loves Me	38
John Brown's Baby	39
Limericks	40
London Bridge Is Falling Down	41
Mary Had a Little Lamb	42
Michael Finnegan	43
Mighty Lak' a Rose	44
Mr. Frog Went A-Courting	46
The Muffin Man	48
My Bonnie Lies Over the Ocean	50
Ninety-Nine Bottles of Beer	49
On the Bridge of Avignon	54
Polly Wolly Doodle	52
Pop! Goes the Weasel	55
Raisins and Almonds	56
Rig-a-Jig-Jig	57
Ring Around the Rosie	58
Rock-a-Bye Baby	59
Row, Row, Row Your Boat	60
Sailing, Sailing	61
She'll Be Coming 'Round the Mountain	62
Sing a Song of Sixpence	66
Skip to My Lou	64
This Old Man	67
Three Blind Mice	68
Twinkle, Twinkle, Little Star	69
Where, Oh Where, Has My Little Dog Gone?	70
Ukulele Chord Dictionary	71

4

A-B-C

Moderately ♩ = 120

TRADITIONAL

A - B - C, tum - ble down G,

cat's in the cup - board but he don't see me.

A-HUNTING WE WILL GO

(To the tune of "The Farmer in the Dell")

By THOMAS ARNE

Verse 2:
A-hunting we will go, A-hunting we will go,
We'll catch a bear and curl his hair,
And then we'll let him go.
(To Chorus:)

Verse 3:
A-hunting we will go, A-hunting we will go,
We'll catch a deer and pull his ear,
And then we'll let him go.
(To Chorus:)

Verse 4:
A-hunting we will go, A-hunting we will go,
We'll catch a moose and Mother Goose,
And then we'll let them go.
(To Chorus:)

Verse 5:
A-hunting we will go, A-hunting we will go,
We'll catch some sheep when they're asleep,
And then we'll let them go.
(To Chorus:)

Verse 6:
A-hunting we will go, A-hunting we will go,
We'll catch a cow and spotted sow,
And then we'll let them go.
(To Chorus:)

Verse 7:
A-hunting we will go, A-hunting we will go,
We'll catch a frog behind a log,
And then we'll let him go.
(To Chorus:)

ALL THE PRETTY LITTLE HORSES

TRADITIONAL

ALL THROUGH THE NIGHT

TRADITIONAL

THE ALPHABET SONG

(To the tune of "Twinkle, Twinkle, Little Star")

TRADITIONAL

ANGELS WATCHING OVER ME

TRADITIONAL

Verse 2:
Sun is setting in the west,
Angels watching over me, my Lord.
Sleep, my child, and take your rest,
Angels watching over me.
(To Verse 3:)

THE ANIMAL FAIR

Moderately ♪ = 120

TRADITIONAL

BAA, BAA, BLACK SHEEP
(To the tune of "Twinkle, Twinkle, Little Star")

TRADITIONAL

THE BEAR CLIMBED OVER THE MOUNTAIN

(To the tune of "For He's a Jolly Good Fellow")

TRADITIONAL

Moderately fast ♪ = 130

1. The bear climbed o-ver the moun-tain, the bear climbed o-ver the moun-tain, the
2.- 4. *See additional lyrics*

bear climbed o-ver the moun-tain to see what he could see.____ 2. He see.____

Verses 2 & 4:
He saw another mountain,
He saw another mountain,
He saw another mountain
And that's what he could see.

Verse 3:
He climbed that other mountain,
He climbed that other mountain,
He climbed that other mountain
To see what he could see.
(To Verse 4:)

BILL HOGAN'S GOAT

TRADITIONAL

Verse 2:
One day that goat
Was feeling fine,
Ate three red shirts
Right off the line.
His master came,
Gave him a whack,
And tied him to
A railroad track.

Verse 3:
The whistle blew,
The train was nigh,
The poor goat knew
That he might die.
He gave three shrieks
Of mortal pain,
Coughed up the shirts
And flagged the train.

BILLY BOY

TRADITIONAL

Verse 2:
Did she bid you to come in,
Billy Boy, Billy Boy?
Did she bid you to come in,
Charming Billy?
Yes, she bade me to come in
There's a dimple in her chin,
She's a young thing and cannot leave her mother.

Verse 3:
Can she bake a cherry pie,
Billy Boy, Billy Boy?
Can she bake a cherry pie,
Charming Billy?
She can bake a cherry pie
Quick's a cat can wink its eye,
She's a young thing and cannot leave her mother.

Verse 4:
How old is she,
Billy Boy, Billy Boy?
How old is she,
Charming Billy?
Three times six and four times seven,
Twenty-eight and eleven,
She's a young thing and cannot leave her mother.

BINGO

TRADITIONAL

Each time the song is repeated, successively substitute a clap for one of the letters of Bingo's name.
1st time: CLAP-I-N-G-O; 2nd time: CLAP-CLAP-N-G-O; 3rd time: CLAP-CLAP-CLAP-G-O, etc.
Last time: substitute all letters with clapping.

BLUE JAY PULLED
THE FOUR-HORSE PLOW

TRADITIONAL

Verse 2:
Saturday night and Sunday too,
True love on my mind.
Monday morning come around,
And then we'll rise and shine.
(Hum)

BOBBY SHAFTO

TRADITIONAL

BRAHMS' LULLABY
(Cradle Song)

By JOHANNES BRAHMS

Moderately ♩ = 100

Lul - la - by, and good - night, with ros - es be -

dight, with lil - ies o'er spread, is ba - by's wee

bed. Lay thee down now and rest, may thy slum - ber be

blessed, lay thee down now and rest, may thy slum - ber be blessed.

COME LITTLE LEAVES

Words by GEORGE COOPER

TRADITIONAL MELODY

1. "Come lit - tle leaves," said the wind one day, "Come o - ver the mead-ow with
2.3. *See additional lyrics*

me and play. Put on your dress - es of red and gold,

Sum - mer is gone and the days grow cold." o - ver their heads.

Verse 2:
Soon as the leaves heard the wind's loud call,
Down they came fluttering, one and all;
Over the brown fields they danced and flew,
Singing the soft little songs they knew.

Verse 3:
Dancing and twirling the little leaves went,
Winter had called them and they were content;
Soon fast asleep in their earthly beds,
The snow laid a soft mantle over their heads.

DID YOU EVER SEE A LASSIE?

(To the tune of "Ach! Du Lieber, Augustin")

TRADITIONAL

Verse 2:
Did you ever see a laddie,
A laddie, a laddie,
Did you ever see a laddie
Go this way and that?
Go this way and that way,
Go this way and that way.
Did you ever see a laddie
Go this way and that?

Alternate Lyric:
The more we get together,
Together, together,
The more we get together
The happier we'll be.
'Cause your friends are my friends,
And my friends are your friends.
The more we get together
The happier we'll be.

DO YOUR EARS HANG LOW?

Moderately ♩ = 120

TRADITIONAL

Verse 2:
Do your ears flip-flop?
Can you use 'em as a mop?
Are they stringy at the bottom?
Are they curly at the top?
Can you use 'em for a swatter?
Can you use 'em for a blotter?
Do your ears flip-flop?

Verse 3:
Do your ears stick out?
Can you wiggle 'em about?
Can you flap 'em up and down
As you fly around the town?
Can you shut 'em up for sure
When you hear an awful bore?
Do your ears stick out?

Verse 4:
Do your ears stand high?
Do they reach up to the sky?
Do they droop when they are wet?
Do they stiffen when they're dry?
Can you summon o'er your neighbor
With a minimum of labor?
Do your ears stand high?

THE FARMER IN THE DELL

TRADITIONAL

Verse 2:
The farmer takes a wife,
The farmer takes a wife,
Heigh-ho, the derry-o,
The farmer takes a wife.

Verse 3:
The wife takes a child,
The wife takes a child,
Heigh-ho, the derry-o,
The wife takes a child.

Verse 4:
The child takes a nurse,
The child takes a nurse,
Heigh-ho, the derry-o,
The child takes a nurse.

Verse 5:
The nurse takes a dog,
The nurse takes a dog,
Heigh-ho, the derry-o,
The nurse takes a dog.

Verse 6:
The dog takes a cat,
The dog takes a cat,
Heigh-ho, the derry-o,
The dog takes a cat.

Verse 7:
The cat takes a rat,
The cat takes a rat,
Heigh-ho, the derry-o,
The cat takes a rat.

Verse 8:
The rat takes a cheese,
The rat takes a cheese,
Heigh-ho, the derry-o,
The rat takes a cheese.

Verse 9:
The cheese stands alone,
The cheese stands alone,
Heigh-ho, the derry-o,
The cheese stands alone.

FATHER'S WHISKERS

Quickly ♩ = 180

TRADITIONAL

1. We have a dear old father for whom we dai-ly

2.-5. *See additional lyrics*

pray, he's got a set of whisk-ers, they're al-ways in the way. They're

al-ways in the way, the cows eat them for hay, they hide the dirt on

pa-pa's shirt they're al-ways in the way. 2. We in.

Verse 2:
We have a dear old brother,
He's got a Ford machine,
He uses Father's whiskers
To strain the gasoline.
To strain the gasoline,
To strain the gasoline,
He uses Father's whiskers
To strain the gasoline.

Verse 3:
Around the supper table,
We make a merry group,
Until dear Father's whiskers
Get tangled in the soup.
Get tangled in the soup,
Get tangled in the soup,
Until dear Father's whiskers
Get tangled in the soup.

Verse 4:
When Father's in a tavern,
He likes his lager beer,
He pins a pretzel on his nose
To keep his whiskers clear.
To keep his whiskers clear,
To keep his whiskers clear,
He pins a pretzel on his nose
To keep his whiskers clear.

Verse 5:
When Father goes in swimming,
No bathing suit for him,
He ties his whiskers 'round his waist,
And then he jumps right in.
And then he jumps right in,
And then he jumps right in,
He ties his whiskers 'round his waist
And then he jumps right in.

FOUND A PEANUT

(To the tune of "Clementine")

TRADITIONAL

1. Found a pea-nut, found a pea-nut, found a pea-nut just now, found a
2.-6. *See additional lyrics*

pea-nut, found a pea-nut, found a pea-nut just now. 2. Broke it now.

Verse 2:
Broke it open, broke it open,
Broke it open just now,
Broke it open, broke it open,
Broke it open just now.

Verse 3:
It was rotten, it was rotten,
It was rotten just now,
It was rotten, it was rotten,
It was rotten just now.

Verse 4:
Ate it anyway, ate it anyway,
Ate it anyway just now,
Ate it anyway, ate it anyway,
Ate it anyway just now.

Verse 5:
Got a bellyache, got a bellyache,
Got a bellyache just now,
Got a bellyache, got a bellyache,
Got a bellyache just now.

Verse 6:
Called the doctor, called the doctor,
Called the doctor just now,
Called the doctor, called the doctor,
Called the doctor just now.

GO IN AND OUT THE WINDOW

TRADITIONAL

Go in and out the win-dow, go in and out the win-dow, go

in and out the win-dow, as we have done be-fore.

Make up additional verses, for example:

Let's strum the ukulele,
The guitar and mandolin.
We'll pick a little banjo
As we laugh and sing.

Let's have some milk and cookies,
Let's have some milk and cookies,
Let's have some milk and cookies,
And then we'll have some more.

FRÈRE JACQUES

TRADITIONAL

Moderately fast ♩ = 140

𝄋 *Chorus:*

Frè - re Jac - ques, Frè - re Jac - ques, dor - mez vous? Dor - mez vous?

To Coda ⊕

Son - nez les ma - ti - nes, son - nez les ma - ti - nes. Ding, din, dong! Ding, din, dong!

Verse:

1. Are you sleep - ing, are you sleep - ing, Broth - er John? Broth - er John?
2. *See additional lyrics*

Morn - ing bells are ring - ing, morn - ing bells are ring - ing.

Frère Jacques - 2 - 1

Verse 2:
Wake up! Wake up! Wake up! Wake up!
Brother John! Brother John!
Ring the morning matins,
Ring the morning matins,
Ding, dang, dong!
Ding, dang, dong!
(To Chorus:)

GOODBYE, MY LOVER, GOODBYE

TRADITIONAL

Moderately ♪ = 130

1. The ship is sail - ing down the bay, good - bye,* my lov - er, good - bye,_____ we
2. *See additional lyrics*

may not meet for man - y a day, good - bye, my lov - er, good - bye. Sing - ing

Chorus:

by - low, my ba - by,

by - low, my bounc - ing ba - by boy, sing - ing

*When sung as a lullaby, try substituting the word "goodnight" for "goodbye" and "baby" for "lover."

Goodbye, My Lover, Goodbye - 2 - 1

by - low my ba - by,_____ good - bye, my lov - er, good-

bye, good-bye, good - bye, my lov - er, good - bye. 2. My bye.

Verse 2:
My heart will ever more be true,
Goodbye, my lover, goodbye,
Tho now I sadly bid you adieu,
Goodbye, my lover, goodbye.
(To Chorus:)

GOODNIGHT, LADIES
(To the tune of "Merrily We Roll Along")

Briskly ♩ = 175

TRADITIONAL

Verse:

1. Good night, la - dies, good night, la - dies, good night, la - dies, we're go - ing to leave you now.

2.-4. See additional lyrics

Chorus:

1.-3. Mer - ri - ly we roll a - long, roll a - long, roll a - long.

4. See additional lyrics

Mer - ri - ly we roll a - long, o'er the dark blue sea. night.

Verse 2:
Farewell, ladies,
Farewell, ladies,
Farewell, ladies,
We're going to leave you now.
(To Chorus:)

Verse 3:
Sweet dreams, ladies,
Sweet dreams, ladies,
Sweet dreams, ladies,
We're going to leave you now.
(To Chorus:)

Verse 4:
Sweet dreams, baby,
Sweet dreams, baby,
Sweet dreams, baby,
It's time to say goodnight.

Chorus 4:
Softly now we go to sleep,
Go to sleep, go to sleep,
Gently now we go to sleep,
It's time to say goodnight.

HERE WE GO 'ROUND THE MULBERRY BUSH

TRADITIONAL

There are many add-on lyrics. Here are just a few.

This is the way we wash our clothes,
Wash our clothes, wash our clothes.
This is the way we wash our clothes
So early Monday morning.

This is the way we iron our clothes,
we iron our clothes, we iron our clothes.
This is the way we iron our clothes
So early Tuesday morning.

This is the way we mend out clothes,
we mend out clothes, we mend out clothes.
This is the way we mend out clothes
So early Wednesday morning.

Sweep the floor…

Scrub the floor…

Wash our face…

Comb our hair…

Shine our shoes…

Go to school…

Brush our teeth…

Bake our bread…

Clap our hands…

HICKORY DICKORY DOCK

Moderately ♪ = 120

HUSH, LITTLE BABY

TRADITIONAL

Verse 2:
If that mockingbird word won't sing,
Mama's gonna buy you a diamond ring.

Verse 3:
If that ring is made of brass,
Mama's gonna buy you a looking glass.

Verse 4:
If that looking glass gets broke,
Mama's gonna buy you and ox and yoke.

Verse 5:
If that ox and yoke turn over,
Mama's gonna buy you a dog named Rover.

Verse 6:
If that dog named Rover runs away,
Mama's gonna buy you a horse and sleigh.

Verse 7:
If that horse and sleigh break down,
You'll still be the cutest little baby in town.

I HAVE A LITTLE DREIDEL

S. E. GOLDFARB

IF YOU'RE HAPPY
(And You Know It)

Easy swing ♩ = 110 (♫ = ♪³♪) TRADITIONAL

1. If you're hap-py and you know it clap your hands. If you're
2.- 6. *See additional lyrics*

hap-py and you know it clap your hands. If you're hap-py and you know it then your

hands will sure-ly show it, if you're hap-py and you know it clap your hands. 2. If you're feet.

Verse 2:
If you're happy and you know it, WIGGLE YOUR EARS.
If you're happy and you know it, wiggle your ears.
If you're happy and you know it
Then your ears will surely show it,
If you're happy and you know it, wiggle your ears.

Verse 3:
If you're happy and you know it, BLINK YOUR EYES.
If you're happy and you know it, blink your eyes.
If you're happy and you know it
Then your eyes will surely show it,
If you're happy and you know it, blink your eyes.

Verse 4:
If you're happy and you know it, TOUCH YOUR NOSE, etc.

Verse 5:
If you're happy and you know it, PULL YOUR EARS, etc.

Verse 6:
If you're happy and you know it, STAMP YOUR FEET, etc.

IT'S RAINING, IT'S POURING

TRADITIONAL

ITSY BITSY SPIDER

TRADITIONAL

JESUS LOVES ME

Words by
ANNA BARTLETT WARNER

TRADITIONAL HYMN

JOHN BROWN'S BABY

TRADITIONAL

LIMERICKS

TRADITIONAL

Quickly ♩ = 175

1. There once was a la-dy from Ni - ger,_____ who

2.-7. *See additional lyrics*

rode on the back of a ti - ger._____ They re - turned from a ride, with the

la-dy in - side, and a smile on the face of the ti - ger._____ 2. There___

Verse 2:
There once was two cats from Kilkenny,
Each thought that was one cat was too many.
So they started to fight,
And to scratch and to bite,
Now instead of two cats there aren't any.

Verse 3:
There once was a man from Peru,
Who dreamed he was eating his shoe.
He awoke in the night
With a terrible fright,
And found it was actually true.

Verse 4:
A mouse in her room woke Miss Dowd,
She was frightened it must be allowed,
But a happy thought hit her
To scare off the critter,
She sat up in the bed and meowed.

Verse 5:
There once was a girl who said, "Why
Can't I look in my ear with my eye?
If I put my mind to it,
I surely can do it,
You never can tell till you try."

Verse 6:
There once was a girl in the choir,
Whose voice rang higher and higher,
It reached such a height
It went clear out of sight,
And they found it next day in the spire.

Verse 7:
There was a young lady from Lynn,
Who was so excessively thin,
That when she essayed
To drink lemonade,
She looked down the straw and fell in.

LONDON BRIDGE IS FALLING DOWN

TRADITIONAL

Verse 2:
How shall it be built again, built again, built again?
How shall it be built again,
My fair lady?

Verse 3:
Build it up with gravel and stone, etc.

Verse 4:
Gravel and stone will wash away, etc.

Verse 5:
Build it up with iron and steel, etc.

Verse 6:
Iron and steel will bend and bow, etc.

Verse 7:
Build it up with silver and gold, etc.

Verse 8:
Thieves will steal the silver and gold, etc.

Verse 9:
Then we'll send a man to watch, etc.

MARY HAD A LITTLE LAMB

TRADITIONAL

Verse 2:
Ev'rywhere that Mary went,
Mary went, Mary went,
Ev'rywhere that Mary went
The lamb was sure to go.

Verse 3:
It followed her to school one day,
School one day, school one day.
It followed her to school one day
Which was against the rule.

Verse 4:
It made the children laugh and play,
Laugh and play, laugh and play.
It made the children laugh and play
To see a lamb at school.

MICHAEL FINNEGAN

TRADITIONAL

Verse 2:
There was an old man and his name was Finnegan,
He went fishing with a pinnegan,
Caught a fish and threw it in again,
Poor old Michael Finnegan.

Verse 3:
There was an old man and his name was Finnegan,
He grew fat and then grew thin again,
Then he died and had to begin again,
Poor old Michael Finnegan.

Verse 4:
I had a cat and his name was Finnegan,
He had whiskers on his chinnegan,
He'd want out and then want in again,
My old kitty cat Finnegan.

MIGHTY LAK' A ROSE

Words by FRANK LEBBY STANTON
Music by ETHELBERT NEVIN

Mighty Lak' a Rose - 2 - 2

MR. FROG WENT A-COURTING

TRADITIONAL

Moderately fast ♩ = 150

1. Mister Frog went a-court-ing and he did ride, ah hah, ah hah, Mister Frog went a-court-ing and he did ride, ah hah, ah hah, Mister Frog went a-court-ing and he did ride, a sword and pis-tol by his side, ah hah, ah hah, ah hah._____ 2. He ___

2.- 9. *See additional lyrics*

1.- 8. │ 9.

Mr. Frog Went A-Courting - 2 - 1

Verse 2:
He rode up to Miss Mousie's door, ah hah, ah hah,
He rode up to Miss Mousie's door, ah hah, ah hah,
He rode up to Miss Mousie's door, gave three knocks and then one more,
Ah hah, ah hah, ah hah.

Verse 3:
He said, "Miss Mousie are you within?" ah hah, ah hah,
He said, "Miss Mousie are you within?" ah hah, ah hah,
She said, "Mr. Frog I sit and spin, just lift the latch and please come in."
Ah hah, ah hah, ah hah.

Verse 4:
He put Miss Mousie upon his knee, ah hah, ah hah,
He put Miss Mousie upon his knee, ah hah, ah hah,
He put Miss Mousie on his knee, he said, "Missy Mouse will you marry me?"
Ah hah, ah hah, ah hah.

Verse 5:
"Without my Uncle Rat's consent, ah hah, ah hah,
Without my Uncle Rat's consent, ah hah, ah hah,
Without my Uncle Rat's consent I wouldn't marry the president."
Ah hah, ah hah, ah hah.

Verse 6:
Where will the wedding supper be? ah hah, ah hah,
Where will the wedding supper be? ah hah, ah hah,
Where will the wedding supper be? Way down yonder in a hollow tree.
Ah hah, ah hah, ah hah.

Verse 7:
What will the wedding supper be? ah hah, ah hah,
What will the wedding supper be? ah hah, ah hah,
What will the wedding supper be? Two green beans and a black-eyed pea.
Ah hah, ah hah, ah hah.

Verse 8:
They all went swimming across the lake, ah hah, ah hah,
They all went swimming across the lake, ah hah, ah hah,
They all went swimming across the lake, they all got swallowed by a big black snake.
Ah hah, ah hah, ah hah.

Verse 9:
There's bread and cheese upon the shelf, ah hah, ah hah,
There's bread and cheese upon the shelf, ah hah, ah hah,
There's bread and cheese upon the shelf, if you want any more you better get it yourself.
Ah hah, ah hah, ah hah.

THE MUFFIN MAN

TRADITIONAL

Verse 2:
Yes, I know the muffin man,
The muffin man, the muffin man.
Yes, I know the muffin man
Who lives in Drury Lane.

Verse 3:
Yes, we know the muffin man,
The muffin man, the muffin man.
Yes, we know the muffin man
Who lives in Drury Lane.

NINETY-NINE BOTTLES OF BEER

Easy swing ♩ = 120

TRADITIONAL

And so on, counting backwards and reducing the number of bottles by one each time.

MY BONNIE LIES OVER THE OCEAN

Moderately fast ♩ = 150

Verse:

SCOTTISH TRADITIONAL

1. My Bon - nie lies o - ver the o - cean,_____ my
2. *See additional lyrics*

Bon - nie lies o - ver the sea,_____ my

Bon - nie lies o - ver the o - cean,_____ oh,

bring back my Bon - nie to me._____

My Bonnie Lies Over the Ocean - 2 - 1

Chorus:

Bring back, bring back, oh, bring back my Bon - nie to

me, to me! Bring back, bring back, oh,

bring back my Bon - nie to me._____ 2. Oh, ___

Verse 2:
Oh, blow the winds over the ocean,
Oh, blow the winds over the sea,
Oh, blow the winds over the ocean,
And bring back my Bonnie to me.
(To Chorus:)

A fun group activity for this song is divided into two parts:

Part 1) When the word "Bonnie" is first sung, everyone stands. As the song continues, everyone
sits down on the word "Bonnie." This action is repeated until the end of the song, standing
up and sitting down.

Part 2) Now the song begins again. When a word beginning with "B" is sung, everyone stands. When
the next "B" is sung, everyone sits down. This action is repeated until the end of the song, up
and down.

The song at first may be sung slowly. As it repeats, it gets faster and faster until absolute chaos results!

My Bonnie Lies Over the Ocean - 2 - 2

POLLY WOLLY DOODLE

TRADITIONAL

Polly Wolly Doodle - 2 - 1

Verse 2:
Oh, my Sal she is a maiden fair,
Sing Polly wolly doodle all the day,
With curly eyes and laughing hair,
Sing Polly wolly doodle all the day.
(To Chorus:)

Verse 3:
Down behind the barn on my hands and knees,
Sing Polly wolly doodle all the day,
I thought I heard a chicken sneeze,
Sing Polly wolly doodle all the day.
(To Chorus:)

Verse 4:
He sneezed so hard with the whooping cough,
Sing Polly wolly doodle all the day,
He sneezed his head and tail right off,
Sing Polly wolly doodle all the day.
(To Chorus:)

Verse 5:
Oh, a grasshopper sitting on a railroad track,
Sing Polly wolly doodle all the day,
A-picking his teeth with a carpet tack,
Sing Polly wolly doodle all the day.
(To Chorus:)

ON THE BRIDGE OF AVIGNON
(Sur Le Pont D'Avignon)

TRADITIONAL

Verse 2:
On the bridge at Avignon,
Soldiers dancing, soldiers dancing,
On the bridge at Avignon,
Soldiers dancing round and round.

Verse 3:
On the bridge at Avignon,
Ladies dancing, ladies dancing,
On the bridge of Avignon,
Ladies dancing round and round.

Verse 4:
On the bridge at Avignon,
Children dancing, children dancing,
On the bridge at Avignon,
Children dancing round and round.

POP! GOES THE WEASEL

TRADITIONAL

Verse 2:
Ev'ry night when I get home
The monkey's on the table,
Go get a stick and knock him off,
Pop! goes the weasel.

Verse 3:
A penny for a spool of thread,
A penny for a needle,
That's the way the money goes,
Pop! goes the weasel.

Verse 4:
Mary's got the whooping cough
And Dicky's got the measels,
That's the way the money goes,
Pop! goes the weasel.

Verse 5:
Half a pound of tuppeny rice,
Half a pound of treacle,
Mix it up and shake it twice,
Pop! goes the weasel.

RAISINS AND ALMONDS

Words and Music by
ABRAHAM GOLDFADEN

RIG-A-JIG-JIG

TRADITIONAL

RING AROUND THE ROSIE

TRADITIONAL

ROCK-A-BYE BABY

TRADITIONAL

ROW, ROW, ROW YOUR BOAT

TRADITIONAL

Moderately ♩ = 110

Row, row, row your boat gen - tly down the stream, mer - ri - ly, mer - ri - ly, mer - ri - ly, mer - ri - ly, life is but a dream.

SAILING, SAILING

Moderately fast ♪ = 150

TRADITIONAL

SHE'LL BE COMING 'ROUND THE MOUNTAIN

TRADITIONAL

Moderately ♩ = 110

1. She'll be com-ing 'round the moun-tain when she comes,_____ she'll be
2.- 5. *See additional lyrics*

com-ing 'round the moun-tain when she comes,_____ she'll be

com-ing 'round the moun-tain, she'll be com-ing 'round the moun-tain, she'll be

com-ing 'round the moun-tain when she comes._____ 2. She'll be ___

She'll Be Coming 'Round the Mountain - 2 - 1

Verse 1:
She'll be coming 'round the mountain when she comes, (TOOT, TOOT)
She'll be coming 'round the mountain when she comes, (TOOT, TOOT)
She'll be coming ' round the mountain, she'll be coming 'round the mountain,
She'll be coming 'round the moutain when she comes. (TOOT, TOOT)

Verse 2:
She'll be pulling six white horses when she comes, (WHOA, HORSE)
She'll be pulling six white horses when she comes, (WHOA, HORSE)
She'll be pulling six white horses, she'll be pulling six white horses,
She'll be pulling six white horse when she comes. (WHOA, HORSE)

Verse 3:
We'll all come out to meet her when she comes, (HOWDY DOO)
We'll all come out to meet her when she comes, (HOWDY DOO)
We'll all come out to meet her, we'll all come out to meet her,
We'll all come out to meet her when she comes. (HOWDY DOO)

Verse 4:
She'll be wearing wool pajamas when she comes, (SCRATCH, SCRATCH)
She'll be wearing wool pajamas when she comes, (SCRATCH, SCRATCH)
She'll be wearing wool pajamas, she'll be wearing wool pajamas,
She'll be wearing wool pajamas when she comes. (SCRATCH, SCRATCH)

Verse 5:
She'll have to sleep with Grandma when she comes, (SNORE, SNORE)
She'll have to sleep with Grandma when she comes, (SNORE, SNORE)
She'll have to sleep with Grandma, she'll have to sleep with Grandma,
She'll have to sleep with Grandma when she comes. (SNORE, SNORE)

And then as a grand finale:
TOOT, TOOT
WHOA, HORSE
HOWDY DOO
SCRATCH, SCRATCH
SNORE, SNORE

SKIP TO MY LOU

TRADITIONAL

Moderately ♩ = 120

1.Flies in the but-ter milk, shoo fly shoo, flies in the but-ter-milk, shoo fly shoo,
2.- 7. *See additional lyrics*

flies in the but-ter-milk, shoo fly shoo, skip to my Lou, my dar - ling.

Lou, Lou, skip to my Lou, Lou, Lou, skip to my Lou,

Lou, Lou, skip to my Lou, skip to my Lou, my dar - ling. dar - ling.

Skip to My Lou - 2 - 1

Verse 2:
Lost my partner, what'll I do?
Lost my partner, what'll I do?
Lost my partner, what'll I do?
Skip to my Lou, my darling.

Verse 3:
I'll find another one prettier than you,
I'll find another one prettier than you,
I'll find another one prettier than you,
Skip to my Lou, my darling.

Verse 4:
Little red wagon painted blue,
Little red wagon painted blue,
Little red wagon painted blue,
Skip to my Lou, my darling.

Verse 5:
Cat's in the cream jar, what'll I do,
Cat's in the cream jar, what'll I do,
Cat's in the cream jar, what'll I do,
Skip to my Lou, my darling.

Verse 6:
Come again, skip to my Lou,
Come again, skip to my Lou,
Come again, skip to my Lou,
Skip to my Lou, my darling.

Verse 7:
Dog ate my pancakes, what'll I do?
Dog ate my pancakes, what'll I do?
Dog ate my pancakes, what'll I do?
Skip to my Lou, my darling.

SING A SONG OF SIXPENCE

TRADITIONAL

Verse 2:
The king was in his counting house, counting out his money,
The queen was in the parlor eating bread and honey.
The maid was in the garden hanging out the clothes,
When down came a blackbird and pecked off her nose.

THIS OLD MAN

TRADITIONAL

Verse 2:
This old man, he played TWO,
He played knick, knack on my shoe, etc.

Verse 3:
This old man, he played THREE,
He played knick-knack on my tree, etc.

Verse 4:
This old man, he played FOUR,
He played knick-knack on my door, etc.

Verse 5:
This old man, he played FIVE,
He played knick-knack on my hive, etc.

Verse 6:
This old man, he played SIX,
He played knick-knack on my sticks, etc.

Verse 7:
This old man, he played SEVEN,
He played knick-knack up in heaven, etc.

Verse 8:
This old man, he played EIGHT,
He played knick-knack on my gate, etc.

Verse 9:
This old man, he played NINE,
He played knick-knack on my vine, etc.

Verse 10:
This old man, he played TEN,
Then he started all over again, etc.

THREE BLIND MICE

TRADITIONAL

TWINKLE, TWINKLE, LITTLE STAR

Lyrics by JANE TAYLOR

TRADITIONAL LULLABY

Moderately ♩ = 130

WHERE, OH WHERE, HAS MY LITTLE DOG GONE?

Words and Music by
SEPTIMUS WINNER

Lively ♩ = 175

Where, oh where, has my lit - tle dog gone? Oh

where, oh where, can he be?_____ With his

ears cut short and his tail cut long, oh

where, oh where, can he be?_____

UKULELE
CHORD
DICTIONARY

A CHORDS

A

2 1

A

4fr.
3 1 2 1

Amaj7

2fr.
1 3 3 3

A6

2fr.
1 3 1 4

Am

2

Am

2fr.
1 3 4 2

Am7

Am6

2 3

A7

2 1 3

A7

1 3 2 4

A9

1 3

A13

1 2 3

Asus

2 3

A7sus

2

Adim7

1 3 2 4

A+

3 1 2

B♭ (A♯) CHORDS*

B♭
3 2 1 1

B♭
3fr.
1 2 4 3

B♭maj7
3fr.
1 3 3 3

B♭6
3fr.
1 3 1 4

B♭m
3 1 1 1

B♭m
3fr.
1 3 4 2

B♭m7
1 1 1 1

B♭m6
2 1 3 1

B♭7
1 2 4 1

B♭7
3fr.
1 3 2 4

B♭9
1 2 1 3

B♭13
1 2 3 4

B♭sus
2 3 1 1

B♭7sus
1 3 4 1

B♭dim7
1 3 2 4

B♭+

4 3 2 1

*B♭ and A♯ are two names for the same note.

B CHORDS

C CHORDS

 C

 C 3fr.

 Cmaj7

C6

 Cm

 Cm 3fr.

 Cm7

Cm6

 C7

 C7

 C9 3fr.

 C13 3fr.

 Csus

 C7sus 3fr.

 Cdim7

 C+

C♯ (D♭) CHORDS*

*C♯ and D♭ are two names for the same note.

D CHORDS

D
1 1 2

D 5fr.
3 2 1 1

Dmaj7
1 1 1 3

D6
1 1 1 1

Dm
2 3 1

Dm 5fr.
3 1 1 1

Dm7
2 3 1 4

Dm6
2 3 1 4

D7
2 3

D7
1 1 1 2

D9
1 3 1 2

D13 5fr.
1 2 3 3

Dsus 2fr.
1 1 2 4

D7sus
2 4

Ddim7
1 3 2 4

D+
4 2 3 1

E♭ (D♯) CHORDS*

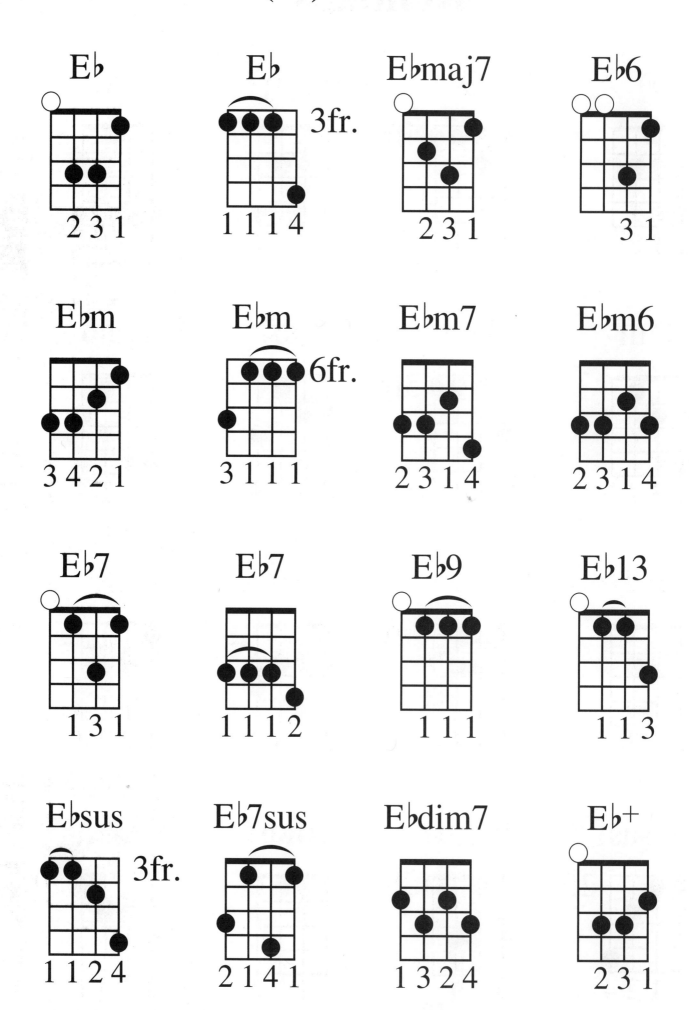

*E♭ and D♯ are two names for the same note.

E CHORDS

F CHORDS

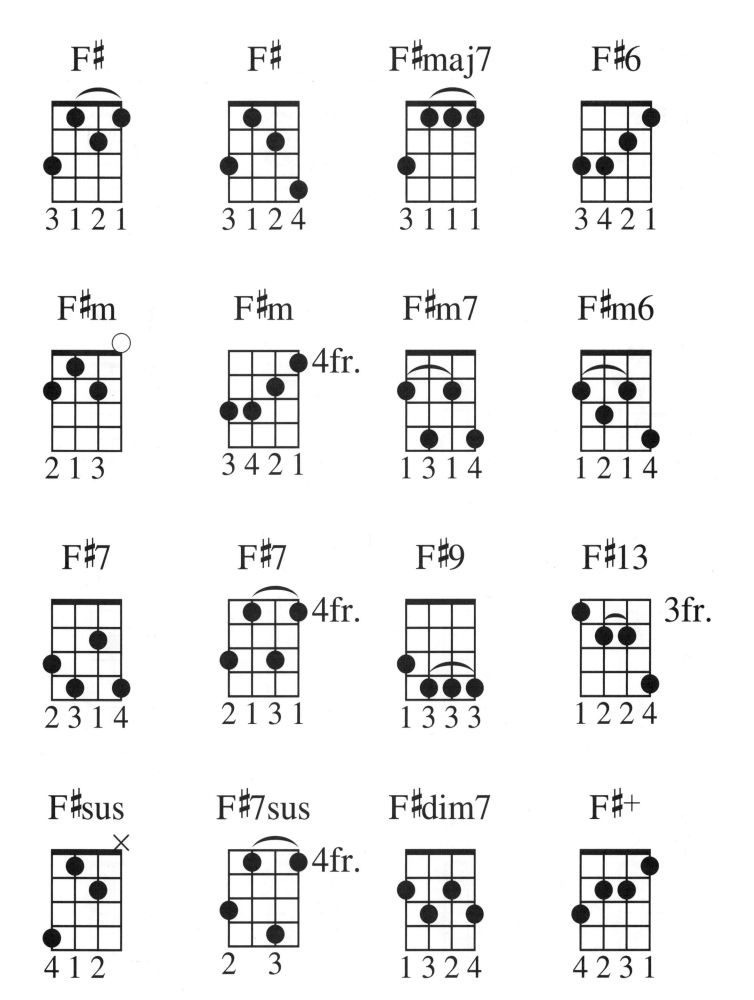

*F♯ and G♭ are two names for the same note.

G CHORDS

Ab (G♯) CHORDS

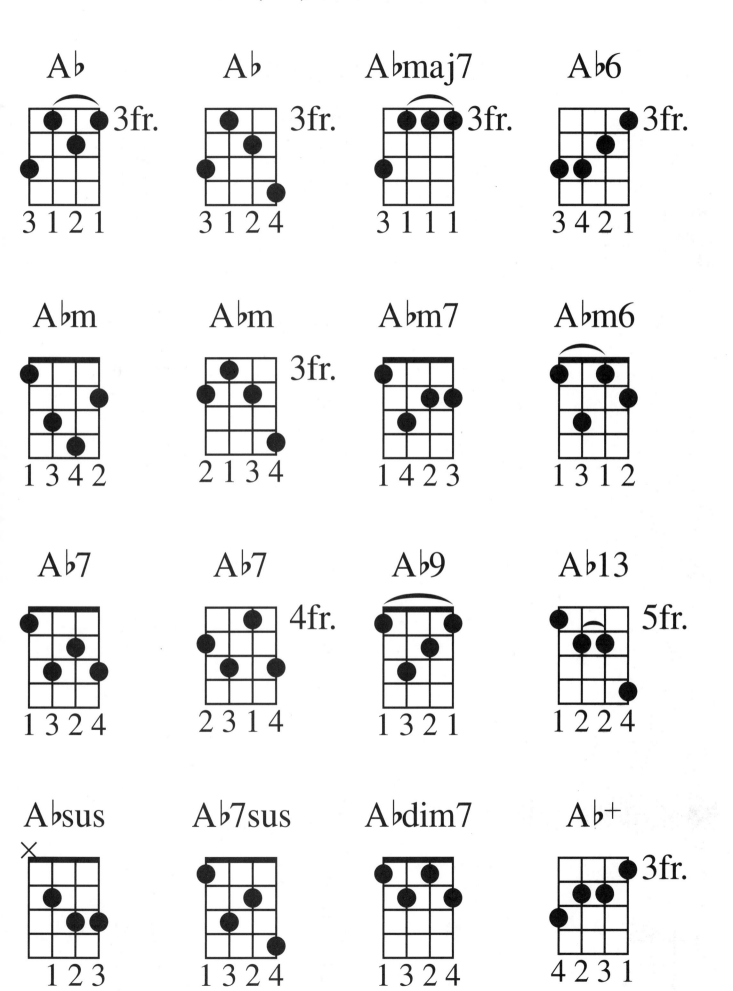

*Ab and G♯ are two names for the same note.